Careers for Creative People

Careers in
Fashion

Peggy J. Parks

ReferencePoint
Press®

San Diego, CA

For more information, contact:
ReferencePoint Press, Inc.
PO Box 27779
San Diego, CA 92198
www.ReferencePointPress.com

LIBRARY OF CONGRESS CATALOGING-IN-PUBLICATION DATA

Name: Parks, Peggy J., 1951– author.
Title: Careers in Fashion/by Peggy J. Parks.
Description: San Diego, CA: ReferencePoint Press, Inc., 2020. | Series: Careers for Creative People | Includes bibliographical references and index. | Audience: Grades 9 to 12.
Identifiers: LCCN 2019018548| ISBN 9781682826805 (eBook) | ISBN 9781682826799 (hardback)
Subjects: LCSH: Fashion—Vocational guidance—Juvenile literature.

Contents

A Passion for Fashion

For young people who are creative, it is natural to dream about careers that revolve around their talents. A high school student who enjoys drawing, for instance, may dream about becoming an illustrator, whereas a classmate who loves to write may long for a career as a novelist. But creative careers expand far beyond drawing and writing, as education counselor Pankaj Kumar explains on the website Quora: "People associate creativity with the arts like writing a novel, painting a picture, or composing music. These are all creative jobs, but not all creative individuals are artists." Many jobs that require creative minds have nothing to do with the arts, says Kumar, who adds, "Creativity simply means being able to come up with something new." One industry that is all about coming up with "something new" is fashion—and it offers a vast array of career possibilities.

A Word with Many Meanings

People throughout the world are intrigued and fascinated by fashion, although how it is defined often differs from person to person. Some use it as a synonym for *style*, and others associate fashion with the latest clothing, shoes, and accessories. Caroline Daniels, who teaches entrepreneurship in London, which is one of the top fashion capitals of the world, refers to fashion as a combination of science and art, as she explains in an article on the LinkedIn website. "[Fashion is the] clothes and accessories we need, and the way we express who we are individually and socially, how we feel, how we wish to communicate," she says. "Fashion communicates

4

values and tastes, thoughts and ideas, form and function, how we work, how we play, joie de vivre . . . and sometimes, just fun."

People thinking about fashion may imagine the dazzling, star-studded fashion shows held in New York City, Paris, and Milan, in which statuesque runway models parade the very latest designer apparel. Thoughts of fashion may also bring to mind gorgeous clothing in colorful spreads in fashion magazines, or new spring or fall fashion collections displayed on the racks of department stores and boutiques. Most people, however, do not realize how much effort it takes behind the scenes to make a fashion show come together, hold a photography session, or get fashions ready for retail sale. In order for these and other aspects of the fashion industry to happen, a huge number of steps and processes must be carried out by a massive number of people.

A World of Opportunity

Worldwide, fashion is a mind-boggling $4.2 trillion industry that employs more than 60 million people. Some of the best-known fashion professionals are fashion designers, who conceptualize and create bold and exciting new fashion collections; fashion photographers; fashion models; editors, like the well-known Anna Wintour, editor-in-chief of *Vogue*; and stylists, whose job is to make celebrities look their very best at all times, from glitzy society events to appearances on the red carpet. But as highly publicized as these fashion professionals are, they represent only a small percentage of fashion industry employment.

Other fashion-related workers include textile designers, pattern makers, tailors, buyers, and fashion trend forecasters. Event planners may work for the fashion industry, and so may sales representatives, fashion merchandisers, visual merchandisers, and public relations specialists. Other fashion professionals include fashion illustrators, graphic designers, fashion journalists—the list goes on and on. For anyone who wants to work in fashion, there is an exciting and diverse array of careers from which to choose.

Yet many young people are not aware of all the career opportunities in the fashion industry. This was true for Nayiri Mampourian,

Careers in Fashion

Occupation	Minimum Educational Requirement	Salary Range
Boutique owner	Bachelor's degree	$0 to $100,000+ (losses are expected for the first few years)
Clothing pattern maker	Formal education at a fashion school	$11,000–$150,000
Costume designer	Bachelor's degree	$32,150–$124,780
Fashion colorist	Postsecondary degree	$32,150–$124,780
Fashion designer	Bachelor's degree	$33,910–$135,490
Fabric librarian	Bachelor's degree	$30,000–$81,130
Fashion merchandiser	Formal education at a fashion school	$32,881–$116,750
Fashion public relations specialist	Bachelor's degree	$20,000–$100,000+
Fashion sales representative	No formal education required	$15,000–$100,000+
Fashion stylist	Postsecondary degree	from $100 daily to $100,000+ a year
Product manager	Bachelor's degree	$45,000–$90,000+
Retail store manager	High school diploma	$15,000–$100,000+
Sample maker	Postsecondary degree	minimum of $12 an hour
Textile artist	Postsecondary degree	$35,000–100,000+

Source: FashionSchools,"Careers," 2019. www.fashion-schools.org.

who is now senior fashion editor for the media, marketing, and consumer brands company Clique in Los Angeles, California. As a teen, Mampourian assumed that the only way she would be able to work in fashion was to become a fashion designer. In an article in the online fashion magazine *Who What Wear*, she writes, "Growing up, I was *dead set* on becoming a designer. Blame it on my *Barbie Fashion Designer* PC game, but I was so laser-focused on what I wanted that I sketched my prom dress when I was 10."

By the time she graduated from college and was looking for jobs, Mampourian had a change of heart about her career focus within the fashion industry. "It turned out I wasn't great at designing," she says, "despite creating the chicest ensembles for my Barbies. But I *did* have an eye for fashion trends and writing about them." That realization inspired Mampourian to switch from fashion design to fashion writing, and her career plan was born. She encourages young people to research the wide variety of careers in fashion to learn about the numerous opportunities that exist.

Dare to Dream

Young people have so much on their minds these days and such packed schedules that it can seem impossible to see beyond the next final exam, let alone spend time thinking about future careers. But time passes quickly, and there is much to be gained by doing some research about possible career ideas. Those who are creative and are passionate about fashion have plenty of choices and opportunities. Some options may not be the right fit, but others may be well worth checking out. "Explore your options," says the New York City fashion recruiting firm Fashion Network on its website. "Doing so will allow you to learn about a variety of careers within fashion so that you can choose the one that is right for you." Fashion Network offers encouraging words for young people who may be thinking about fashion careers. "Nowadays it can be rare to be in a situation where going to work doesn't feel like work. Luckily, getting into fashion allows you to do what you love every day of the week. At the same time, it has the potential to take you to places you've only dreamed of."

Fashion Designer

What Does a Fashion Designer Do?

Fashion designers are artistic, creative individuals who are able to envision fashions and then transform their ideas into finished products. They often specialize in a particular type of fashion, such as clothing, footwear, accessories, or costumes. Clothing designers create apparel, including casual wear, suits and other business attire, sportswear, outerwear (such as jackets and coats), evening wear (including elegant gowns), maternity clothing, and intimate apparel. Footwear designers specialize in a variety of shoes and boots for all occasions and seasons of the year. Accessory designers specialize in purses and tote bags, along with belts, scarves, hosiery, and hats. Costume designers create costumes for actors to wear in live theater productions, movies, and television programs.

Fashion designers have a wide variety of duties and tasks. They are ultimately responsible for every aspect of bringing fashions to the people who buy them. Although the exact design process often varies by specialty, it typically

At a Glance

Fashion Designer

Minimum Educational Requirements
Bachelor's degree

Personal Qualities
Artistic talent, creativity, attention to detail, communication skills, computer design software skills, good business sense

Working Conditions
Hectic schedules can be stressful; long hours often required; frequent travel, sometimes outside the United States

Salary Range
About $33,910 to $135,490 per year

Number of Jobs
About 23,800 as of 2016

Future Job Outlook
Growth of 3 percent through 2026

takes six months from the time initial design concepts are created to final production, when either spring or fall fashion collections are released.

The first step in this long, complex process is research, which often involves studying trend reports published by fashion industry trade groups. These reports offer predictions about the anticipated popularity of styles, colors, and fabrics for an upcoming season. On the basis of their research, as well as their own inspiration, fashion designers begin to sketch what they have envisioned. Many still do the initial sketches by hand and then scan them into a computer with computer-aided design (CAD) software such as Adobe Illustrator or Photoshop. This software enables designers to view their fashion concepts on animated models on the screen. Designers can experiment with different colors, designs, and patterns to determine how their conceptual fashions will actually look. CAD software also allows fashion designers to see how their clothing fits and moves as the virtual models walk, run, and twirl on the screen. According to what they observe, fashion designers can make any necessary modifications to their designs. This is much easier, less time consuming, and less expensive than making adjustments with real fabrics on real models.

Once the CAD work is done, the fashion designer is ready to develop a working pattern. This often involves creating a toile (pronounced "twall"), which is a rough mockup of the design made of inexpensive fabric like muslin. By placing the toile on a mannequin, the designer can see how it will fit and drape on a person. In the documentary Signé Chanel, legendary fashion designer Karl Lagerfeld speaks about how essential a toile is for the design process. "The toile is used to work out the proportions, the shoulders, the lengths, etc," he says. "If you use the real fabric right away you may not get a good fit. It's risky, so it's better to work from a basic structure or pattern that's discarded when the dress is cut. The toile gives you the proportions and an idea of the finished product, so you can avoid making mistakes."

The final phase of the fashion design process is production. Although most fashion designers are experienced in sewing, they rarely sew their own designs unless they are just getting started in their careers and/or work in very small design firms. Typically, fashions are produced in garment factories located in the United States or other countries. When the fashions are complete, they may be displayed by runway models in fashion shows and then offered to the public for sale.

How Do You Become a Fashion Designer?

Education

Most fashion designers hold an associate's or bachelor's degree in fashion design or fashion merchandising. These programs feature drawing classes as well as classes in design, art history and fashion history, sewing and pattern making, apparel construction, textiles and fabrics, and CAD, among others. The National Association of Schools of Art and Design accredits approximately 350 colleges and universities that offer programs in art and design, and many of these schools offer fashion design programs.

One of the most prestigious of these programs is offered by the Fashion Institute of Technology (FIT) in New York City. The FIT program is extremely challenging, which is evident in its dropout rate of more than 60 percent. Nicholas Rissone, a FIT graduate and aspiring fashion designer, writes candidly about how tough the program is in an article on spoiled.NYC, a New York City food and culture website. "Trust me," says Rissone, "a disgruntled professor coming over and saying 'this is all wrong you need to start over' happens more than you may think." He says students typically have a heavy class load, attending seven to ten classes per week with each lasting from two to four hours. And according to Rissone, homework is a given. "Fashion design students' lives REVOLVE around homework," he says. Yet as tough as it is, Rissone says that for those who truly love fashion design, the schooling is a "labor of love." He writes, "You have to LOVE the idea of creating beautiful clothes, and pushing through every all-nighter, sewing machine malfunction, and every 'it's time to start over.'"

A fashion designer does her preliminary sketches on paper. When they are done, she will scan them into a computer and use the latest software to complete them.

Hands-On Experience

Aspiring fashion designers can gain valuable work experience by participating in an internship program with a clothing manufacturer, fashion design firm, or fashion stylist. An internship is often required as part of a college fashion design curriculum. In its online career publication, the Bureau of Labor Statistics (BLS) explains, "Internships provide aspiring fashion designers an opportunity to experience the design process, building their knowledge of textiles and colors and of how the industry works." Also, those who want careers in fashion design should spend time creating a portfolio, which is a collection of their best design concepts. The BLS says that fashion design students often have opportunities to enter their designs in contests, which helps them develop their portfolios.

Skills and Personality

A number of skills are essential for those who want to be fashion designers—such as artistic talent and creativity. "Do you like to draw?" asks career counselor Penny Loretto in an article on the Balance Careers website. "If so, that's good news because you're going to need this skill as you pursue being a fashion designer. Strong drawing skills are a must in fashion, as designers need to be able to take a concept and get it down on paper." Other important skills include a good eye for detail; an understanding of texture, color, and fabric; excellent communication and interpersonal skills; proficiency in using CAD software; and the ability to work with a team.

Also, says Loretto, fashion designers must have a thorough understanding of business. "Creativity is the essence of fashion, but without a good understanding of business, it is difficult to sustain a fashion brand and make it profitable," she says. "Many talented fashion designers have ended up bankrupt because they had a poor understanding of fashion's financial side."

On the Job

Employers

In 2016 fashion designers in the United States held about 23,800 jobs at a variety of locations. About 20 percent of them are self-employed, while others work for wholesale or manufacturing establishments, apparel companies, retailers, theater or dance companies, or fashion design firms. Most US fashion designers work in the major fashion hubs of New York City and Los Angeles. Those who would rather work outside the United States typically choose the European fashion capitals of London, Paris, and Milan.

Working Conditions

Fashion design is a high-pressure, competitive career, in which the term *typical day* does not apply. "There's no such thing," says fashion designer Cynthia Rowley in a March 2018 interview on the *USA Today* website. Rowley goes on to describe the volatility of her work environment. "It's really like a bombardment of stimulation," she says. "It's really hectic, but exciting. It's loud and creative. . . . It's so fast-paced that every element of the creative process is happening simultaneously every day."

Fashion designers often work long hours to meet production deadlines and to prepare for upcoming fashion shows. Those who work independently on a freelance basis tend to work longer hours to adapt their workday to the schedules and deadlines of their clients, which often means working nights and weekends. Travel is a typical part of a fashion designer's job. Designers visit suppliers, manufacturers, and customers throughout the United States and in other countries. Many travel several times a year to trade shows and fashion shows to learn about the latest fashion trends.

With such an enormous number of responsibilities, fashion designers tend to have extremely hectic schedules. Yet most love what they do and could not imagine doing anything else. This is true of fashion designer Sandy Liang, whose fun, colorful, upbeat fashions are popular with a host of celebrities, including Victoria's Secret models Kendall Jenner and Elsa Hosk. "It's nice to bring a little bit of happiness to somebody via these clothes," Liang says in a February 2018 interview with *Glamour*. "I love it when people try on a jacket and they smile—I'm like, Job done."

Earnings

A fashion designer's salary can vary widely, depending on experience, proven talent, and recognition of work. As of May 2017, salaries for fashion designers ranged from about $33,900 to more than $135,490 per year. With a median annual wage of $67,420, these professionals earn significantly more than those who work in other types of art and design occupations.

Opportunities for Advancement

Aspiring fashion designers must be prepared to work hard to succeed in their chosen career. They often begin by working for experienced designers in jobs such as sketching assistant or pattern maker. Career planning expert Dawn Rosenberg McKay writes in an article on the Balance Careers website, "In due course, you can become a chief designer or a design department head, but that will be after accumulating many years of experience."

What Is the Future Outlook for Fashion Designers?

According to the BLS, employment of fashion designers is projected to grow 3 percent through 2026, which is slower than the average for all occupations. This amounts to about six hundred new jobs that will be available to fashion designers in the coming years. "Those with formal education in fashion design, excellent portfolios, and industry experience will have the best job prospects," says the BLS. Aspiring fashion designers should expect strong competition for jobs. This will result from the large number of people who desire careers in fashion design all vying for relatively few available positions.

Find Out More

Council of Fashion Designers of America (CFDA)
65 Bleecker St., Eleventh Floor
New York, NY 10012
website: https://cfda.com

The CFDA is a not-for-profit trade organization whose members include more than five hundred of America's foremost fashion designers. The organization has awarded numerous scholarships to undergraduate students, and membership for students includes access to its fashion calendar and members-only events.

Fashion Group International
8 W. Fortieth St., Seventh Floor
New York, NY 10018
website: http://fgi.org

Fashion Group International is a global nonprofit with five thousand members who work in the fashion industry. Its mission is to provide information on the business of fashion and fashion design to its members, helping them become more effective in their careers. Membership provides access to this information, as well as a membership directory and industry events.

Fashion Industry Association (FIA)
18948 N. Dale Mabry Hwy.
Lutz, FL 33548
website: www.thefia.org

The goal of the FIA is to foster cooperative business practices across the fashion industry, including in fashion design, which it aims to achieve through networking via an extensive industry directory. The FIA website includes a blog and information about industry events and meetings worldwide.

National Association of Schools of Art and Design (NASAD)
11250 Roger Bacon Dr., Suite 21
Reston, VA 20190
website: https://nasad.arts-accredit.org

NASAD is an organization of approximately 363 schools, colleges, and universities. The organization sets the standard for design degrees and assists schools and students working to attain education in design. The NASAD website includes a list of commonly asked questions for fashion design students regarding school accreditation, applying to a program, and more.

Visual Merchandiser

What Does a Visual Merchandiser Do?

The creative, fashion-savvy people who work in visual merchandising are responsible for how fashions are displayed in retail stores and boutiques. They organize clothing displays throughout a store, style and dress mannequins, and create attractive, inviting window displays. And this merchandise presentation is not done at random. Rather, it is meticulously planned to be appealing to shoppers and increase sales. Avi Keswani, cofounder and director of the LISAA School of Design in Paris, writes: "As a shopper, we probably don't realize the influence the merchandising strategy has on our buying decisions. Everything we see inside our favorite shops, from the visual displays and signage to mannequins' attire and placement, to the balance of coordinating outfits and the organization of every single piece of apparel and product on a store's floor, is all carefully planned by the store's merchandising team for the ideal fashion consumer experience."

At a Glance

Visual Merchandiser

Minimum Educational Requirements
High school diploma or equivalent

Personal Qualities
Creativity, good eye for detail, ability to work independently, effective communication skills, professionalism, analytical skills

Working Conditions
Typically inside retail stores; early morning and late night hours often required, as well as some weekends and holidays; some travel required

Salary Range
About $36,000 to $54,000 per year

Number of Jobs
About 120,870 as of May 2017

Future Job Outlook
Growth of 2.5 percent through 2026

A key member of the merchandising team is the visual merchandiser. Also known as merchandise presentation managers, visual merchandising specialists, merchandise displayers, or other similar titles, these professionals' jobs revolve around the same basic goal: stimulating fashion sales through strategic presentation of merchandise displays.

In small retail operations or boutiques, visual merchandisers—who are often the owners—usually design their own fashion displays. In the case of large retailers that may have hundreds of stores nationwide, decisions about merchandise presentation are made at the corporate level, which ensures that fashions are displayed consistently from store to store. Corporate visual merchandising teams develop comprehensive plans for exactly how fashions should be displayed in stores. The displays are typically planned around a particular theme, such as holidays or seasons of the year. Once plans are complete, they are furnished to stores for implementation by local visual merchandisers.

This is the process followed by major fashion retailer Old Navy, which is headquartered in San Francisco. Each month the corporate merchandising staff prepares what is known as the *Style Guide*, which is sent to more than eleven hundred stores throughout North America. The printed guide is very specific about how each department must be represented. It provides detailed information about how to place merchandise, what visuals to use, and how mannequins should be dressed, among other directions. Full-color detailed photos support the text and illustrate exactly how merchandise should look. The guide also specifies a deadline for when the presentation changes must be completed and the displays in place.

Along with creating fashion displays on a store's sales floor, visual merchandisers also spend time on office work. Those employed by large retailers with multiple store locations often share fashion news and other information with stores via email, telephone, text message, and/or videoconference technology.

They may prepare budgets, write requisitions for new store signage, and place orders for items that a store may need. When Lily Alegria was a visual merchandising coordinator at the retailer Lucy Activewear, one of the tasks she worked on during office hours was helping plan the layouts of stores that were scheduled for remodeling. She also ordered accessories and fixtures for those stores, including chandeliers, decor, mannequins, and signage. "In my position there are a lot of interior design aspects, which I love but was not expecting," Alegria says in an interview on the *AfterCollege* blog. "I never thought I would be picking out chandeliers for stores or putting together seating areas!"

Visual merchandisers may also be involved in training activities, especially at large retailers with multiple store locations. As the chief point of contact for new merchandise plans, visual merchandisers must communicate the corporate office's directions to local visual merchandising team members and store associates. In an article on the Balance Careers website, retail industry expert Barbara Farfan writes, "You will help train the store team about design concepts, visual display standards, and the property maintenance of the overall visual display effort. By providing on-the-job training, feedback, and recognition, you will motivate other members of the store team to support your visual merchandising efforts actively."

How Do You Become a Visual Merchandiser?

Education

Although education requirements vary according to an employer's individual specifications, entry-level visual merchandisers typically need only a high school diploma or equivalent. But those with a college degree may have a better chance of being hired and are often paid more than people with no advanced education. "A degree in Visual Merchandising gets your foot in the door," Alegria says in her interview on the *AfterCollege* blog.

One immensely popular school among aspiring visual merchandisers is New York City's Fashion Institute of Technology (FIT). It offers a program called Visual Presentation and Exhibition Design, which features both two- and four-year degrees. The program is very wide ranging. It includes a variety of art and business courses, as well as job-specific classes in mannequin presentation, visual presentation for in-store design, lighting design, interpretive exhibition design, and interpretive exhibition graphics, among others. Along with classroom instruction, students work on actual projects, creating large-scale window displays that are exhibited in one of the city's busiest blocks.

Hands-On Experience

Because work experience is as, or even more, valuable to employers than education, aspiring visual merchandisers can benefit from participating in internship programs. These programs provide invaluable benefits, from firsthand experience on the job to networking with prominent leaders in the fashion industry who could potentially become employers.

Aspiring visual merchandisers who are enrolled in college programs may be required to do one or more internships. This is true at FIT, which requires an internship for almost all its programs, including Visual Presentation and Exhibition Design. On its website, the institute describes some internship opportunities and explains the benefits: "You may intern with companies such as Ralph Lauren, Guess, Liz Claiborne, Nike, Macy's, Ann Taylor, JC Penney, Perry Ellis, Ross Stores, and Saks. Internship opportunities with these retailers, apparel manufacturers, or showrooms grant credits towards your degree, offer a rewarding work experience and often result in a full-time position after graduating."

In March 2019 the major fashion retailer Nordstrom advertised online for a visual merchandiser intern at its Schaumburg, Illinois, location. "As a Visual Merchandiser intern, you'll play a dual role—part dedicated student, part visual expert," the ad explains. The internship is paid, as most are, and lasts for eight weeks. The intern's responsibilities include helping build, install, and take down store promotional displays and window presentations; ensuring that the store is compliant with corporate signage programs and proper safety guidelines; planning and implementing store promotional campaigns and activities along with the store team; and helping train, coach, and give daily feedback on garment presentation to the store staff.

Skills and Personality

People who thrive in visual merchandising positions are those who possess a unique combination of qualities. They need creativity and also must have a good eye for detail. They must have excellent organizational skills and be effective communicators. Farfan offers advice for aspiring visual merchandisers: "In smaller retail operations, you will likely be the one-person visual merchandising department and, therefore, you will need [to] be self-reliant, self-motivated, and . . . achieve goals and meet deadlines without supervision." Farfan adds that visual merchandisers who work in larger stores will likely be executing plans developed by others. So the ability to follow written and verbal instructions, with great attention to detail, is essential.

Being a visual merchandiser also requires business savvy and analytical skills. Displays must not only be attractive and appealing, they must also entice customers to buy merchandise, or the displays are ineffective. Also essential for visual merchandisers, says Alegria, is the ability to take criticism of their work. "You have to have thick skin," she says, "since you are putting your work on display constantly." Also, says Alegria, visual merchandisers must be in good physical condition because it is hard work to move merchandise around and create displays. "It is also a very physical world, which they never told me in school," she says. "You are on high ladders, carrying around heavy mannequins, you are moving heavy fixtures. You need to be tough."

On the Job

Employers

As of May 2017 visual merchandisers in the United States held about 120,870 jobs at a variety of locations. Most are employed by retail chains and large department stores, such as Lord & Taylor, Macy's, Bergdorf Goodman, Nordstrom, and others. Visual merchandisers may also work for event management companies or agencies that provide contract services to retail establishments that do not have their own in-house visual merchandising teams.

Working Conditions

In general, visual merchandisers spend their time inside retail establishments where they are arranging merchandise displays. Doing major fashion moves may require some early morning and late night hours, as well as weekend work. Depending on the position, visual merchandisers may spend some of their time traveling. And as Alegria noted, the job is often physically demanding.

Earnings

The salary for visual merchandisers in the United States ranged from about $36,000 to $54,000 per year as of February 2019. Salaries can vary widely, depending on factors such as education, years of experience, and proven track record on the job. Another factor in salary levels is the size of the employer and geographic location. At the upscale New York City fashion retailer Neiman Marcus, for example, a visual manager job posted on Glassdoor paid up to $88,000 per year. At Macy's in New York City, the position paid up to $75,000 per year.

Opportunities for Advancement

Visual merchandisers are often initially hired as assistants or coordinators and then work their way up the career ladder. Those who excel in their jobs may be promoted to management positions and/or be transferred to major cities, where they can gain valuable experience and earn more money.

What Is the Future Outlook for Visual Merchandisers?

According to the Bureau of Labor Statistics, employment of visual merchandisers is projected to grow 2.5 percent through 2026, which is slower than the average for all occupations. This amounts to about 3,022 new jobs that will be available in the coming years. The most opportunities for visual merchandising positions will be with larger retailers, especially those in major cities such as New York, Chicago, and Los Angeles.

Visual merchandising is not for everyone, but for those with the right skills and motivation, it may be a great career choice. It is never boring, there is always something new to learn, and working in a bustling retail environment can be both challenging and exciting. Farfan refers to visual merchandising positions as "popular, coveted, competitive and viewed as being one of the 'fun jobs' that the retail industry has to offer."

Find Out More

design:retail
website: www.designretailonline.com

This website offers industry events, daily headlines, and project case studies. The organization also hosts GlobalShop, the largest annual trade show in the United States for visual merchandisers, as well as producing the *design:retail* print magazine, which features articles about the latest developments in the retail industry.

National Retail Federation (NRF)
1101 New York Ave. NW, Suite 1200
Washington, DC 20005
website: www.nrf.com

The NRF is the world's largest retail trade organization. Its website includes a newsletter and a jobs board. Membership is available for retailers and industry partners, as well as universities and their students. Membership in the NRF provides resources to support education, research, and careers in the retail industry.

Retail Design Institute
126A W. Fourteenth St., Second Floor
Cincinnati, OH 45202
website: www.retaildesigninstitute.org

The Retail Design Institute works with colleges and universities to develop degree programs in retail design. Membership is available for students and industry professionals and provides access to networking events and a jobs board. The organization also sponsors store-designing competitions for professionals and students.

Visual Merchandising and Store Design (VMSD)
website: www.vmsd.com

The VMSD provides retail designers with innovative store-design ideas, marketing strategies, and industry news and events. Students can view a wide variety of design galleries and competitions, as well as subscribe to the online *VMSD* magazine.

Fashion Stylist

What Does a Fashion Stylist Do?

Fashion stylists are highly creative, style-savvy professionals whose work revolves around making their clients look their absolute best from head to toe. They have a diverse range of tasks that can vary widely, depending on their specialty and the clients they serve.

Their titles may also vary. As well as fashion stylists, they may be known as fashion consultants, wardrobe stylists, personal stylists, or celebrity stylists.

One of the most essential parts of a stylist's job is understanding a client's personality, unique needs, and personal style challenges. In an article on the Fashionista website, Los Angeles–based stylist Andrea Lublin discusses her initial consultation with clients: "I'll go to them and talk about what they're looking for, what their needs are and look at their stuff to get a feel for their aesthetic — what they like, the colors that work for them, the fit and what makes them feel comfortable or uncomfortable."

At a Glance

Fashion Stylist

Minimum Educational Requirements
No requirement; associate's or bachelor's degree recommended

Personal Qualities
Creativity, an eye for style, extensive knowledge of fashion trends and brand names, knowledge of fashion history, excellent communication skills, empathy, social media marketing skills

Working Conditions
Typically indoors in comfortable temperatures; working long hours, nights, weekends, and holidays typical; often high stress due to deadlines and unpredictable client temperaments

Salary Range
About $22,455 to more than $112,000

Number of Jobs
About 23,800 as of 2016*

Future Job Outlook
Growth of 3 percent through 2026*

* Based on Bureau of Labor Statistics estimates for fashion designers

Once stylists have a good idea what a client is looking for, they can begin shopping for wardrobe pieces. They shop at all kinds of stores, often depending on a client's budget. Lublin has developed relationships with salespeople at high-end department stores like Saks Fifth Avenue and Barneys New York, so she frequents these stores, as well as shopping online. Stylists also purchase items from consignment shops, thrift shops, and vintage stores. Leesa Evans, who is a personal stylist and costume designer in Los Angeles, frequents vintage retailers when shopping for her clients. She also taps into her costume-design resources to build custom wardrobe pieces for some of them.

After shopping, stylists schedule a fitting. This could take place at the client's home, in the stylist's office, or in a special area at a department store. Amanda Schwartz, a personal stylist in Nashville, Tennessee, works for the fashion retailer Nordstrom, and that is where she meets clients for their fittings. "Before they come in for the consultation, I will set up a fitting room that includes all aspects of a good, buildable wardrobe," Schwartz says in a Fashionista article. "Then, we work together to try everything on and find items that accommodate their personal style, as well as needs and wants."

Fashion stylists often emphasize that working with their clients is about a lot more than just the wardrobe. This is true of Laurel Kinney, a personal stylist and wardrobe consultant in Austin, Texas, whose background is not typical for a stylist. She has a master's degree in social work and was a social worker in New York City and Austin before becoming a stylist. Kinney says there is a close relationship between psychology and styling, as she explains in an interview with the online publication *Tribeza*. "I always say, it's 80 percent psychology and only 20 percent about the clothes, really. So I definitely feel like I look at it differently than just from a straight fashion perspective." Kinney's workdays are packed with activities. "I'm all over the place," she says. Typically, she meets with clients for initial consultations, drives around to clients' homes to evaluate their wardrobes, shops for client fashions, and has client fittings.

Many of the same tasks described by Kinney also pertain to celebrity stylists. Micaela Erlanger is a fashion stylist whose clients include actors Lupita Nyong'o, Meryl Streep, and Michelle Dockery. Jamie Mizrahi styles for Katy Perry, Nicole Richie, and Riley Keough. Stylist Karla Welch's clients include Justin Bieber, Elisabeth Moss, and Tracee Ellis Ross. And Ilaria Urbinati, known as Hollywood's premier men's stylist, has a star-studded client list that includes Bradley Cooper, Rami Malek, John Krasinski, Donald Glover, Armie Hammer, and Jimmy Fallon. These and other celebrity stylists emphasize the importance of developing a close, trusting relationship with clients. Because of the nature of their positions, celebrities are often wary of people they do not know, especially when letting them take care of something as intimate as personal styling.

How Do You Become a Fashion Stylist?

Education

Whether aspiring fashion stylists should earn a college degree is largely a matter of personal preference. A college education is not a requirement for being a stylist, but career experts say it is beneficial to have a degree. Many well-known stylists have attended college, such as Erlanger, who received a business degree from Parsons School of Design in New York City, and stylist Erin Walsh, who holds a bachelor of theater arts from New York University's Tisch School of the Arts. Stylist Rachel Zoe earned a bachelor's degree in psychology and says in an interview with the *Los Angeles Times* that she uses her degree "every single day" because of how it helps her better serve her clients. Many stylists agree that having advanced education has helped them in a number of ways, and they recommend college for aspiring stylists.

Hands-On Experience

One thing fashion stylists overwhelmingly agree on is the importance of on-the-job experience, and they emphasize that aspiring stylists should seek out every opportunity to gain that experience. One way to do this is to find professional stylists in their communities and volunteer to assist them at no charge. Another suggestion is offering to style family members or friends who are attending a special event or even just going out for an evening. This was one technique used by Skyler McCurine, who owns a professional styling business called Le Red Balloon in San Diego, California. When she was just starting out as a stylist, McCurine's first client was a friend of her father.

Internships are an excellent way to gain hands-on experience in styling. Interning helps aspiring stylists get a firsthand look at what stylists do day to day, and the experience can be invaluable. When Erlanger was a student at Parsons School of Design, she took any internship that was available, and she recommends that all aspiring stylists do the same. "It was integral to getting me experience and ultimately giving me a breadth of knowledge where I could become an assistant and move up the food chain," she says in an interview with the British edition of Vogue magazine published online. "I interned every single summer and every semester. I treated every internship with the same dedication I did school. . . . I really got a taste of what styling was like on set and in a safe environment where I could contribute."

Skills and Personality

Fashion stylists have a variety of jobs and responsibilities, but there are certain skills and personality traits they all need. They must be highly creative and passionate about fashion, and they must have the desire to keep up-to-date with the latest fashion trends and color schemes. They also need a keen eye for detail. They must be excellent listeners, be patient, and be empathetic with their clients. McCurine discusses the need for empathy in an interview with the Penny Hoarder website. "You don't just see people changing or trying on clothes," she says. "You see their scars, sometimes emotional, sometimes physical. It requires empathy to understand what they're dealing with."

Also essential for fashion stylists are exceptional interpersonal skills; a friendly, outgoing personality; the ability to be flexible and adaptable to frequent, sometimes constant, change; superb organizational skills; the ability to work well independently; and a good business mind-set with an entrepreneurial spirit.

On the Job

Employers

Many fashion stylists work for themselves as independent contractors, or freelancers. They may also be employed by fashion retailers like Nordstrom or Saks Fifth Avenue or by specialty boutiques. Or they may work for styling service companies that employ teams of stylists. One of these companies is BREE JACOBY Inc. in West Hollywood, California. Owned by a stylist of the same name, it is a luxury styling service that specializes in consulting, closet makeovers, personal styling, custom clothing, and in-home tailoring.

Working Conditions

One of the qualities fashion stylists need is flexibility, and that is because their jobs can be so unpredictable. They work in all kinds of environments, including their studios, client homes, and department store consultation rooms or fitting rooms. Those who work with celebrities travel a lot, sometimes jetting from Los Angeles to New York City and Paris within the same week. Stylists who work with celebrities are under a great deal of pressure, and their jobs can be very stressful. People often think of celebrity stylists as having glamorous jobs, but there is a price to pay. They do work closely with famous people, but their jobs are taxing. Chris Horan, who styles for actors Debby Ryan and Rowan Blanchard and model/actor Hari Nef, talks about this in an interview with the fashion industry website Business of Fashion. "What nobody tells you when you're fighting to make it is that it never gets easier," says Horan. "No matter how successful I get, it's always going to be this crazy grind with unpredictable hours and unending stress. But it will always be worth it, because I love what I do and I love my clients."

A fashion stylist works with a client. The stylist's goal is to help her client look her absolute best; she does that by shopping for flattering styles, overseeing fittings, and suggesting alternatives when needed.

Earnings

The wages fashion stylists earn are extremely variable. According to the salary and benefits website PayScale, earnings for this career range from about $22,455 to more than $112,000 per year. Celebrity stylists in Los Angeles and New York can earn hundreds of dollars per hour or per "look," meaning fashion ensembles for a particular event. Horan receives about $500 per look, which can amount to thousands of dollars for one client's multiple appearances, such as events during New York's Fashion Week. But celebrity stylists also have to cover costs such as shipping clothing and accessories cross-country, salaries for assistants, tailoring, and dry cleaning, all of which can significantly reduce their earnings.

Opportunities for Advancement

Fashion stylists who work at department stores or for styling firms may, after working for several years, be able to go out on their own and start their own styling businesses with their own clients. Those who have made a name for themselves will be sought after by additional clients, which will help them grow their client base and focus on higher-level work.

What Is the Future Outlook for Fashion Stylists?

The government agency that tracks career data is the Bureau of Labor Statistics (BLS), and fashion stylist is not a career for which the agency collects data. Although the BLS does not collect data on fashion stylists, data for fashion designers is often used for estimating purposes. The BLS projects 3 percent growth for fashion designers through the year 2026.

Celebrity stylist Mimi Cuttrell offers a rosier projection for stylists. Cuttrell, whose clients include Gigi and Bella Hadid, Ariana Grande, and Priyanka Chopra, says that opportunities for fashion stylists are growing. "Styling as a career will continue to become more in demand!" says Cuttrell in an article in the online fashion magazine *Who What Wear*. "There is so much work to be done, and I hope young people who want to work in fashion will consider styling as a career."

Find Out More

Association of Image Consultants International (AICI)
1000 Westgate Dr., Suite 252
Saint Paul, MN 55114
website: www.aici.org

The AICI is the largest professional organization for image consultants worldwide. The organization provides certification and continuing education and also hosts an annual conference. Its website includes information about industry events, webinars, and certification for image consultants.

Fashion Industry Association (FIA)
18948 N. Dale Mabry Hwy.
Lutz, FL 33548
website: www.thefia.org

The goal of the FIA is to foster cooperative business practices across the fashion industry, which it aims to achieve through networking via an extensive industry directory. The FIA website includes a blog and information about industry events and meetings worldwide.

Fashion Institute of Technology (FIT)
Seventh Ave. at Twenty-Seventh St.
New York, NY 10001
website: www.fitnyc.edu

FIT is an internationally recognized college for students in design, fashion, art, communications, and business. Its rigorous academic program includes academic and industry partnerships. In addition to its on-campus degree programs, the institute offers online courses.

International Association of Professional Image Consultants (IAPIC)
167 Midland Pl. SE
Calgary, AB, Canada T2X 1N1
website: www.iapcollege.com

The IAPIC is part of the IAP Career College program, which offers online certifications for numerous careers, including image consultants. Membership in the program includes course discounts, a newsletter, and a listing in the IAP Professional Directory.

Fashion Illustrator

What Does a Fashion Illustrator Do?

Fashion illustrators are talented, highly skilled artists who use illustration to show new designs or trends in clothing, footwear, and accessories. These illustrations are in demand by national magazines such as *Vogue*, *Elle*, *Harper's Bazaar*, *Cosmopolitan*, and *Glamour*, among others. Fashion illustrators' art also appears in catalogs, books, and advertisements; on product packaging; and on the packages of sewing patterns. "Fashion illustrators and the world of fashion itself often go hand-in-hand," says illustrator Mary Winkler in an article on the creative learning website Envato Tuts+. She goes on to say that fashion illustrators are very much in demand. "Almost any company or client that wants to focus on fashion, fashion design, or fashion-related products may need a fashion illustrator," says Winkler.

Fashion illustrator Jeanette Getrost was in middle school when she decided that she would someday have a career in fashion, although she had no idea what that career might be. "I assumed that you could either be a designer or a model," Getrost says in an interview with *Entrepreneur* that appears on its website. "I didn't really understand the industry, so I would just draw clothing a lot." She loved to draw and was good at it, but combining fashion and drawing into a career did not cross her mind. "I didn't know that fashion illustration was even a thing," she says. Today she is a successful illustrator whose work has been featured in *Vogue*, and she has partnered with brands such as Chanel, Christian Dior, Dolce & Gabbana, Coach, Ferragamo, and Jimmy Choo. She has also done packaging illustration for the Paris-based cosmetics and skin care company Sephora. "There's nothing better than walking into a store and seeing your work," says Getrost.

Fashion illustrators also do live sketching, which involves drawing during a live event, such as a fashion show. Although these events are heavily photographed, fashion illustrators are also hard at work as the models are strutting along the runway. And the demand for these sorts of illustrators is seeing a resurgence, as fashion curator Connie Gray explains in an article on the European luxury publication *Living It*: "Fashion illustration is seriously making a comeback."

Fashion illustrators also live-sketch in other types of venues, such as department stores during a special event. Nicole Jarecz, a fashion illustrator from Detroit, Michigan, does live sketching events for fashion retailers such as Neiman Marcus and Lord & Taylor. "When I do a live sketching event I bring all of my art supplies with me," she says in an interview with the online lifestyle magazine *Seen*. "I have a desk where I set up shop, and then I just wait for people to come by and watch. Shoppers love to stop and see what I'm doing." During these live sketching events, Jarecz creates custom illustrations for shoppers. She might sketch them modeling a piece of clothing or shoes they are trying on or with a new handbag or other accessory they have just purchased. "It's a great way for shoppers to have a one-of-a-kind experience at a store and for them to take home a souvenir," Jarecz explains. She adds that by the time the live sketching event ends, her hands are tired because she has sketched continuously for two to three hours.

In the course of doing their jobs, fashion illustrators use a variety of art tools. Depending on the project and the type of illustration they are creating, they may use colored pencils, graphite pencils, fine black pens, charcoal, markers, or watercolor paints. Many fashion illustrators also use digital drawing technology, such as an iPad tablet computer and a wireless stylus tool known as Apple Pencil. In the blog of the print and design company MOO, New York City fashion illustrator Brooke Hagel talks about digital drawing and says she was intrigued by it for a long time and then "finally took the plunge" in 2016. "It's certainly different and takes some getting used to," she says. "I've tried a variety of drawing apps to experiment in and found different ones work to achieve different effects." And even though there are advantages to using digital drawing, and she will continue to do so, Hagel says, "I'll always go back to traditional art supplies and won't be turning in my pencils, markers or paints anytime soon."

Many fashion illustrators have a strong social media presence, which they say is important for raising awareness of their work among potential clients. Instagram is one of the most popular social media apps among illustrators, including Getrost, who as of April 2019 had more than 105,000 followers. She estimates that about 85 percent of inquiries she receives about her illustrations are from Instagram. The downside, however, is that keeping a social media presence active, updated, and fresh can be time consuming. In the *Entrepreneur* article, Getrost talks about this. "It takes time, in the beginning, especially, if you're getting used to it—you just spend so much time on it," she says. "You have to just dedicate many, many hours to being plugged in, which can feel maybe a little soul-sucking."

How Do You Become a Fashion Illustrator?

Education

Like many fashion illustrators, Getrost has a bachelor's degree, although it is in journalism rather than fine arts. She also took drawing composition classes at a local college and spent a lot of time Googling "fashion illustration" to get a good sense for potential career avenues. According to the Bureau of Labor Statistics (BLS), most fine artists (including illustrators) earn a bachelor's or master's degree in fine arts to sharpen their skills and improve their job prospects. But Winkler says that not all fashion illustrators go to college. They might take art classes to study illustration or fine arts or might develop their skills on their own through years of work experience.

Whether or not aspiring fashion illustrators attend college, professional illustrators urge them to spend as much time as possible learning about fashion and the arts. "Explore many different mediums and ways of working," says Jarecz in the *Seen* interview. "Familiarize yourself with all of the programs out there. Sketch from life. Explore, explore, explore. Look at art every day. Research illustration history. There's so much to learn!" She says it is also important to become familiar with the business of illustration. "You can be the very best illustrator out there, but if you don't know how to market yourself, then you will be lost."

Hands-On Experience

When clients seek fashion illustrators, they look for talent, fashion illustration skills, and a proven track record—which requires years of experience. One of the best ways aspiring fashion illustrators can get on-the-job experience is by participating in internships. These are usually paid positions, and they allow young people to learn from experts while at the same time earning college credits. When Hagel was a student at New York City's Fashion Institute of Technology, she did an internship with the wardrobe departments of *Saturday Night Live* and the popular HBO series *Sex and the City*. This helped broaden her understanding of fashion.

Aspiring fashion illustrators can also gain hands-on experience in other ways. They can join art clubs at their school or become involved with the school yearbook, newspaper, or literary magazine. "These publications often make use of visual art to accompany their text," says an article on the Vault career website. Experience can also be gained through summer part-time work, perhaps assisting a professional artist or working at a fashion boutique. The

Vault article adds, "Explore your interest in the fashion field by reading fashion magazines that will keep you up to date on fashion trends, models, and illustrators' work." Another excellent tactic for aspiring fashion illustrators is to create an online presence by posting their illustrations on social media.

Skills and Personality

Fashion illustrators are people who possess the unique combination of artistic talent and a love of fashion. They must be creative and imaginative, with good interpersonal skills, an excellent eye for detail, and good customer service skills, because they often deal with the public. Also important is being comfortable learning new technology skills, because fashion illustration is often done with digital art tools. Social media skills are also necessary because fashion illustrators often use Instagram or other platforms to display their work. "Share your work!" says Hagel in the online MOO interview. "The only way prospective clients will find you is if your work is out there. Whether it be through your own site, blog, Instagram, Facebook—or the next big social media platform—share it and promote yourself." Those who dream of working for themselves, like Hagel, must be highly organized, savvy about business and marketing, self-motivated, and able to drum up business and manage finances when income is often erratic. "Work seems to come in tidal waves," says Hagel.

On the Job

Employers

Most fashion illustrators work for themselves as independent contractors, or freelancers. They may also be employed by publishing companies, national magazines, design firms, or advertising agencies. In addition, fashion illustrators may work for fashion designers.

Working Conditions

Typically, fashion illustrators work in comfortable, well-lighted conditions inside art studios that are in office buildings, renovated warehouses, or lofts. If they do live sketching, as many fashion illustrators do, they may work at a variety of locations, from inside fashion retail stores to venues where fashion shows are held.

Earnings

According to the salary and benefits website PayScale, annual income for fashion illustrators typically ranges from $21,376 to more than $86,000 per year. The amount they can earn is dependent on their level of talent and skill, their experience, their reputation, and also their location. Jarecz offers some advice for aspiring fashion illustrators in the *Seen* interview: "Don't expect to get rich being an illustrator. Do it because you *love* it. If you love it, then it will show through your work."

Opportunities for Advancement

Fashion illustrators advance in their careers by building a reputation among their clients for being talented and skilled, fashion-savvy, and dependable. As they complete new assignments, they continue to add to their portfolios and have opportunities to attract higher-level, more prestigious clients.

What Is the Future Outlook for Fashion Illustrators?

The BLS does not collect data solely on fashion illustrators but projects 7 percent growth through 2026 for fine artists, a category that includes all illustrators. Many people who are in the fashion industry predict a promising future for fashion illustrators, as Gray explains in the *Living It* article: "Twenty years ago you saw almost no fashion illustration but this is gradually changing as editors are looking for something fresh to draw the eye. There are some extraordinarily talented illustrators working at the moment that are bringing it back into fashion in a big way."

Find Out More

American Institute of Graphic Arts (AIGA)
AIGA National Design Center
233 Broadway, Suite 1740
New York, NY 10279
website: www.aiga.org

The AIGA is the world's oldest professional membership organization for design, including fashion illustration. Membership benefits include a jobs board, webinars, event discounts, and a place to display a portfolio.

Arts of Fashion Foundation
555 California St., Suite 4925
San Francisco, CA 94104
website: www.arts-of-fashion.org

The Arts of Fashion Foundation is a nonprofit for academics and professionals with the goal of fostering creativity and the design process in the fashion industry. The foundation hosts an annual design contest for students, as well as master classes in Paris.

Fashion Institute of Technology (FIT)
Seventh Ave. at Twenty-Seventh St.
New York, NY 10001
website: www.fitnyc.edu

FIT is an internationally recognized college for students in design, fashion, art, communications, and business. Its rigorous academic program includes academic and industry partnerships. In addition to its on-campus degree programs, the institute offers online courses.

Graphic Artists Guild
31 W. Thirty-Fourth St., Eighth Floor
New York, NY 10001
website: https://graphicartistsguild.org

The Graphic Artists Guild advocates for professionals in design, including fashion illustrators. Membership in the guild provides access to webinars, pricing guidelines, social and educational events, and more.

Society of Illustrators
128 E. Sixty-Third St.
New York, NY 10065
website: www.societyillustrators.org

The Society of Illustrators is a nonprofit organization that promotes the art of illustration through exhibitions and lectures. The organization provides a membership for students that includes free admission to its museum, invitations to members-only events, and discounts for lectures, workshops, and more.

Fashion Buyer

What Does a Fashion Buyer Do?

When shoppers walk into a department store or fashion boutique and see the array of beautiful garments, shoes, and accessories, they are probably not wondering where the items came from or how they ended up in the store. They are more likely thinking about which fashions they want to purchase and take home with them to wear. But the fact is, those garments, shoes, and accessories are in the store because they were carefully chosen and purchased by fashion buyers. On its website, the Chegg educational group describes the buyer's role: "You are paid to travel to fashion shows, negotiate with manufacturers, and study the color and cut predictions for the upcoming seasons. You're responsible for deciding that this wedge heel will be stocked in brown and pink, but not blue. On the whole, you get to set the style direction for your brand and help dictate what people will be wearing this season."

Although fashion buyers typically specialize in a certain area, such as women's apparel, menswear, shoes, or accessories, their job responsibilities are basically the same no matter which specialty they choose—and they have a tremendous amount of responsibility. Buyers must be savvy about not only fashion but also the customers who buy the fashions and what they care about. And buyers must also thoroughly understand their companies' brand and values. Buyers regularly analyze sales data and fashion trend forecasts, which tell them what products did or did not sell in the past. This information is then used to help guide buying decisions for the future. This analysis is tricky and requires a unique combination of hard data and personal instinct—as well as the ability to defend buying decisions if necessary. In an interview on the *Girl Got Faith* blog, a fashion buyer from the United Kingdom named Amy talks about this. "There will be times when you have to fight for people to listen to your opinion and you need to be able to justify the decisions you're making," she says. "Sometimes the weirdest item, that other people would normally say is a bad idea, can actually sell really well, and in those circumstances it's the . . . buyer trusting their instincts that has made that happen."

Usually, fashion buyers make their purchases during certain times of the year they call buying seasons, which typically coincide with Fashion Week in major fashion capitals. These are the busiest times, when buyers' days are long and jam-packed with numerous fashion shows, designer showroom meetings, and other activities. On the Grailed website, Alix Rutsey, menswear buyer for the Montreal, Canada, luxury retailer SSENSE, says that on these especially hectic days, she makes sure to dress comfortably. "You'll rarely see me in heels because I'm on my feet all day, running around," she says. "I'm almost always in sneakers or a pair of loafers."

During Fashion Week, which is held in February and September each year in New York City, Paris, London, and Milan, Rutsey goes to as many runway shows as she can. "Shows can be magical and allow you to step into the world the designer worked to create," she says. But as much as she enjoys fashion shows, "the real fun is in the showroom." She says most of her time during buying season is spent meeting with designers in showrooms.

"We work with designers and brands from all over the world," she says, "so fashion weeks are also one of the few opportunities I get to connect with everyone, face to face."

Because fashion buyers make a living by shopping and also spend a great deal of time at fashion shows and in designer showrooms, people might assume they have a glamorous job. Although there is indeed a certain element of glamour to the career, a fashion buyer's job is anything but easy. As British fashion buying consultant Nicole Davidson writes in her blog, "Whilst there's definitely an element of the more fabulous side of life (once you get to the higher levels) there's also a bit more to it than that. It's a ridiculously varied and pressured job role that keeps you on your toes at all times." Working as a buyer is not for everyone, says Davidson, "but it's a great industry for those that really love fashion and have the right balance of skills."

How Do You Become a Fashion Buyer?

Education

Educational requirements for fashion buyers can vary considerably, depending on their employers and the size of the organization. Most businesses require a minimum of a bachelor's degree in business, finance, or a related field because of the analytical nature of a buyer's job. Most fashion buyers have college degrees, and those who pursued fashion buying careers often took a number of fashion-related classes. New York City fashion buyer Chinelo Okona knew from a young age that she someday wanted to work in fashion. When she was working toward her bachelor's degree in business administration at Georgia State University, she worked part-time in retail sales to gain experience in the retail environment and learn more about fashion. When she decided on a career as a fashion buyer, she knew the decision was the right one. "I felt like buying was the perfect marriage of my strong analytic and creative skills in the industry that I've always wanted to break into," she says in an interview with the online magazine *Ms. Vixen*.

Hands-On Experience

Career experts highly recommend that aspiring fashion buyers do what Okona did and work in retail as sales associates. In an article on the Monster website, Fashion Institute of Technology career director Connie Passarella explains why this is excellent preparation for a fashion buying career. "It's not a requirement, but companies like to see retail experience on an individual's resume," she says. "That way, they know you have a basic understanding of the selling floor."

There are numerous other ways that aspiring fashion buyers can gain hands-on experience, with internships among the most valuable. These are typically available to college students and are offered by many retail establishments and businesses during the summer months when students are on break. The positions are often, but not always, paid, and interns can earn college credit while gaining invaluable on-the-job experience. Many young people take advantage of all the internship opportunities they can, often interning every summer during their college years. Veteran fashion buyer Shira Suvoyke, who graduated from Boston University, says in an interview on the HuffPost website, "If you think you want to be a buyer, go work in a retail job, go intern during the summer. Get that experience."

Skills and Personality

Fashion buyers must be passionate about fashion, along with having a good sense for the business side of buying. They must be mathematically inclined and have very strong analytical skills. They need keen intuition, which they will rely on often when making decisions about what is most likely to be popular and sell six months in the future. Buyers also need excellent organizational skills, great communication skills, and the ability to work well with others. In addition, they need good negotiation skills, a competitive spirit, and the ability to handle stress and cope with a high-pressure environment. And, says Suveyke in the HuffPost interview, self-confidence is essential. "If you're not confident in yourself and your opinion of what you're doing, you're going to get lost," she says. "It's definitely not an industry made up of wallflowers."

Employers

Fashion buyers work for large retail chains like Burlington, Claire's, Designer Shoe Warehouse, and JOANN Fabrics; major department stores like Macy's, Barneys New York, Saks Fifth Avenue, and Neiman Marcus; the growing field of online fashion retailers; and boutiques. Typically, buyers work at a company's headquarters, wherever that may be. Often these businesses are headquartered in major cities.

Working Conditions

Fashion buyers work in different locations depending on what task they are working on. When analyzing fashion trends and studying sales data, they work at a computer in their office. They also spend a lot of time outside their office attending fashion shows and going on buying trips to many different cities, internationally as well as in the United States, to meet with designers. According to career consultant Susan Gill, travel can account for 60 percent to 70 percent of a fashion buyer's job. Although fashion buying is an exciting and challenging career, it is also a high-pressure, high-stress job that often requires long hours and extended periods of time away from home.

Earnings

According to the salary and benefits website PayScale, annual salaries for fashion buyers range from $26,825 to $111,744. Earnings can vary considerably, depending on geographic location, the size of the employer, and the buyer's experience level, among other factors.

Opportunities for Advancement

Fashion buyers are usually hired as assistant buyers or junior buyers. As fashion buyers gain knowledge and experience, they may be promoted to associate buyer, then buyer, and then senior buyer. Some large retailers, including Neiman Marcus, offer training programs that enable entry-level buyers to learn on the job and prepare for higher-level positions.

What Is the Future Outlook for Fashion Buyers?

The Bureau of Labor Statistics (BLS) does not collect data specifically about fashion buyers but does collect data about the more general category of wholesale and retail buyers. As of 2016, 123,300 of these professionals were employed throughout the United States. The BLS projects that through the year 2026, there will be a 2 percent decline in wholesale and retail buyer jobs—but that does not necessarily pertain to fashion buying positions, and it should not discourage aspiring fashion buyers from pursuing their career dreams. "Sometimes you just have to go for it!" says *Who What Wear* managing editor Michelle Scanga in an article on the publication's website. "If you're passionate enough about the industry, you will find a way to make it work."

Find Out More

American Collegiate Retailing Association (ACRA)
Department of Marketing
Georgia Southern University
PO Box 8154
Statesboro, GA 30460
website: www.acraretail.org

The ACRA is a professional organization of educators from four-year institutions nationwide that are dedicated to providing quality education in retail and retail management. It holds conferences every year, as well as publishes newsletters about retail education.

American Purchasing Society
8 E. Galena Blvd., Suite 406
Aurora, IL 60506
website: www.american-purchasing.com

The American Purchasing Society is composed of buyers, purchasing managers, and other professionals interested in retail buying from all fifty states and twenty-eight countries. It offers online courses, certification as a Certified Purchasing Professional, and a jobs board and career center for retail buyers.

National Retail Federation (NRF)
1101 New York Ave. NW, Suite 1200
Washington, DC 20005
website: https://nrf.com

The NRF is the world's largest retail trade organization. Its website includes a newsletter and a jobs board. Membership is available for retailers and industry partners, as well as universities and their students. Membership in the NRF provides resources to support education, research, and careers in the retail industry.

Retail Environments
4651 Sheridan St., Suite 470
Hollywood, FL 33021
website: www.retailenvironments.org

Retail Environments magazine provides in-depth analyses on today's retail industry through research, reporting, and thought-leader commentary, as well as the latest products for retail environments and inspiring retail/brand projects.

Fashion Journalist

What Does a Fashion Journalist Do?

The field of journalism is all about keeping the public informed through researching and reporting news and current happenings. Fashion journalists, also called fashion writers or fashion reporters, are part of this field, but they specialize in a particular kind of news: the fashion industry and nearly everything and everyone associated with it. It is the responsibility of fashion journalists to track down and report on new trends and fads, the latest styles for spring or fall, updates from Fashion Week and its star-studded events, up-to-date information about fashion designers and their collections, and the lives and activities of fashion models and other fashion-conscious celebrities. Whatever the news might be, if it relates to fashion, it is up to fashion journalists to inform people about it.

Although glossy print magazines are still popular with those who love fashion, the popularity of digital publications continues to grow. Many fashion journalists write for these online publications, either exclusively or

At a Glance

Fashion Journalist

Minimum Educational Requirements
Bachelor's degree

Personal Qualities
A keen eye for fashion, excellent interpersonal and communication skills, creativity, strong research and writing skills, time-management skills, computer proficiency, persistence, competitiveness

Working Conditions
In an office, as well as various other locations to attend fashion shows and conduct interviews; often long hours and hectic schedules

Salary Range
About $17,000 to $110,500

Number of Jobs
About 131,200 as of April 2018*

Future Job Outlook
Growth of 8 percent through 2026*

* Based on Bureau of Labor Statistics estimates for writers and authors

along with writing for print. Emily Manning, a fashion journalist based in New York City, says that those who are new to fashion writing should expect primarily digital publication assignments, at least at the beginning of their careers. Manning knows from personal experience how valuable such assignments can be, as she explains in an article on the Fashionista website: "Digital content production has taught me so much about how to construct a story. I'm much more confident working on print pieces now that I've had years of digital experience informing the choices I make."

Whether they are writing for print publications or digital magazines, when fashion journalists are assigned a story by an editor, the first step is information gathering. If the assignment is to write about a fashion show, for instance, the journalist attends the show, takes notes, and often meets with designers whose collections are being featured. Afterward, the journalist uses the information he or she has gathered to write the story and send it to an editor for approval or revisions. This can make for a hectic, jam-packed day, especially if a journalist is assigned to cover more than one fashion show.

Sophia Winfield, who is studying fashion journalism at the London College of Fashion, was chosen to cover several fashion shows during London's Fashion Week in February 2019. She attended the first show and then went backstage to meet with featured designers. In an article on the Graduate Fashion Week website, Winfield writes, "After congratulating them on their hard work, I made my way back to the office to write my review." She had very little time to write her story before rushing off to the next fashion show at 2:00 p.m., and then she attended another show at 3:30 p.m. A few hours later she had meetings with several more designers. They showed her their collections and shared with her the inspiration behind them. Following that meeting she hurried back to her office to write up her notes and then left to attend the last show of the day. By 7:30 p.m. she was on her way back to her office to finish writing her articles and send them to her editors. "It was tiring, but worth it," says Winfield.

Aside from attending and writing about fashion shows, fashion journalists may meet independently with fashion designers to interview them for stories. The journalist contacts the designer's representative to set up an appointment for the interview. When that time has been set, the journalist conducts the interview either in person or on the phone. Fashion journalist Eman Bare, who is from Toronto, Canada, was just starting out in her career when she was assigned to interview Kate Spade, a famous designer of handbags and other fashion accessories. Bare had long been a devoted fan of Spade's designs, and she was extremely nervous about the coveted assignment. As she explains in an article on the *Teen Vogue* website, "Here I was, just barely out of journalism school, and about to interview the woman who inspired so much of my life. How did I get this lucky?"

At the agreed-upon time, Bare called Spade's office, assuming that a media contact would answer—and says she nearly fainted when Spade herself answered the phone. Spade was warm and gracious, and Bare's nervousness quickly dissolved. She felt as if she were talking with an old friend rather than a world-famous designer. The interview went beautifully, and Bare wrote her story. Years later, after Spade's tragic suicide, Bare wrote that she still felt grateful to Spade for making her feel important even though she was only a "young journalist desperate to get into the world of fashion writing."

How Do You Become a Fashion Journalist?

Education

Most fashion journalists earn a bachelor's degree. They may choose a fashion-related program or focus on other areas such as business, communications, or journalism. Eva Chen, formerly an editor with *Teen Vogue* who is now with Instagram, says many aspiring fashion journalists think they must major in fashion to work as fashion journalists, but that is incorrect. She explains:

It's definitely not true. There are people who work at *Teen Vogue* who are history, English, political science, and Spanish majors. Everyone comes from different backgrounds, and the common denominator between all the majors is that they teach how to communicate efficiently and effectively. Any major where you're writing a lot, debating, discussing, and learning to express yourself through the written word is the best to have. At the end of the day, the fundamental requirement for working at a magazine is communication, so your major should help forward that skill.

Hands-On Experience

Fashion journalism is a competitive, highly sought-after career field, so those who aspire to become part of it must acquire all the experience they can. Internships are an excellent way to do that. Interning enables aspiring fashion journalists to gain valuable experience in interviewing and writing, as well as allowing them to meet many different people in the fashion industry. "As an aspiring fashion journalist, you can never have too many internships or too much work experience," fashion writer André Wheeler explains in an article on the Fashionista website. "Even if the work is unpaid, the positions will strengthen your writing portfolio and, more importantly, provide useful connections. Unpaid internships can pay off." Wheeler goes on to say that Manning, the New York City fashion journalist, secured a full-time job through the connections she made while interning for a major fashion retailer. Just before she graduated from college, Manning received an offer from one of those connections to work at the online fashion, music, and art magazine *i-D*.

Aspiring fashion journalists can gain experience in many other ways as well, such as starting a blog and writing in it prolifically. They can find interesting people to interview and write about them, and they can attend shows and write up reviews. Fashion journalist Hannah Rogers says that the best advice she ever received was from the managing editor for the publication *British Vogue*. When Rogers said she was a writer and the editor asked about her writing portfolio, Rogers felt embarrassed that she did not have one. "So I started blogging," she says in an article on the Fashionista website, "just to have a digital portfolio to send to commissioning editors and have on my [résumé]."

Skills and Personality

A variety of skills are necessary for fashion journalists to succeed in their jobs. They must love fashion and be able to write about the topic with enthusiasm, clarity, and creativity. They need excellent research skills and the persistence to track down information from a variety of sources—and they must be able to handle the frustration this can sometimes cause. They need good interpersonal skills and excellent communication skills, including listening as well as speaking. Being detail oriented is essential for fashion journalists, as is being organized, self-motivated, and disciplined about meeting deadlines that can seem impossibly tight.

On the Job

Employers

Fashion journalists work for all kinds of publications, including those that publish print magazines and those that are exclusively digital. They may also work for major newspapers such as the *New York Times*, *Chicago Tribune*, and *Los Angeles Times*. The majority of fashion journalists work as freelancers. After a highly successful career working for Michael Kors, *Time* magazine, and *Women's Wear Daily*, Caroline Tell knew it was time to do what she had always wanted to do: write. So she became a freelance fashion journalist. "I knew that my work at Kors, while challenging and exciting, wasn't what I was meant to be doing," says Tell in an interview with the online women's magazine Lifestyle Edit. "I'm so grateful for the education I got in the social and digital space, but I felt I wasn't utilizing my best skills. So, I just took the leap."

Working Conditions

When they are writing, fashion journalists work in an office. They also spend a great deal of time traveling from appointment to appointment, conducting interviews, attending fashion shows, and meeting with editors. A fashion journalist's hours can be long, and schedules are often hectic. Depending on the assignment, fashion journalists may need to travel to other cities, possibly outside the United States. This is an exciting part of the job, especially for newcomers to the field. After years of fantasizing about going to Paris for Fashion Week and attending a Chanel fashion show, the dream came true for Kristen Nichols in the spring of 2018. "Walking into the Grand Palais with my invite tucked under my arm was a surreal pinch-me experience," says Nichols in an article in the online fashion magazine *Who What Wear*.

Earnings

According to the online employment marketplace ZipRecruiter, annual earnings for fashion journalists range from $17,000 to $110,500. This wide variance is due to factors such as geographic location, level of experience, reputation, and whether journalists work for a publication or are freelancers.

Opportunities for Advancement

Fashion journalists who have proved themselves and have built an impressive portfolio may advance to higher-level writing jobs. Or they may have enough credibility and demand for their work that they can start their own businesses. Another logical career move for fashion journalists is to become editors. They would likely start as assistant editors and advance to managing or executive editor positions. Those who become fashion editors are in charge of the overall vision for a fashion publication. They are responsible for what will be featured, including editorial material and photographs, and they delegate assignments to fashion writers and photographers.

What Is the Future Outlook for Fashion Journalists?

The Bureau of Labor Statistics (BLS) does not collect data specifically for fashion journalists. For the broader, more general category of writers and authors, the BLS projects an 8 percent growth in employment through 2026. Although fashion journalists make up only a small number of those writers and authors, economists predict strong growth in the fashion industry in the near future, which is a promising sign.

Find Out More

American Society of Journalists and Authors (ASJA)
355 Lexington Ave., Fifteenth Floor
New York, NY 10017
website: https://asja.org

The ASJA is the nation's largest society for nonfiction authors, including fashion journalists. The society offers access to events, seminars, and workshops. The ASJA website's "For Writers" section provides information about its annual conference, along with an industry podcast.

American Society of Magazine Editors
757 Third Ave., Eleventh Floor
New York, NY 10017
website: https://asme.magazine.org

This organization includes leading editors at many of the nation's consumer and business magazines, including fashion magazines. It offers a Best Cover Contest as well as an internship program for college seniors majoring in journalism.

Association for Women in Communications (AWC)
1717 E. Republic Rd., Suite A
Springfield, MO 65804
website: www.womcom.org

The AWC supports women working in communications, including fashion journalists, by providing a supportive community of women professionals and monthly professional development events. The AWC website also includes a blog and a jobs board.

Fashion Industry Association (FIA)
18948 N. Dale Mabry Hwy.
Lutz, FL 33548
website: www.thefia.org

The goal of the FIA is to foster cooperative business practices across the fashion industry, including in fashion journalism, which it aims to achieve through networking via an extensive industry directory. The FIA website includes a blog and information about industry events and meetings worldwide.

Fashion Trend Forecaster

What Does a Fashion Trend Forecaster Do?

Most people who work in fashion are well acquainted with the term *trend forecasting*, because it plays a big part in what they do for a living. But those who are not fashion industry insiders may have no idea what it is or even that such a thing exists at all. Jane Buckingham, founder of the marketing and trend forecasting firm Trendera, hints at the mystery around trend forecasting during an interview with the online fashion magazine *Who What Wear*. When asked to describe her job, Buckingham replied, "Technically, I am a trend forecaster, research, and generational expert. But even my family doesn't really know what that means!"

Trend forecasters are sharp, analytical, fashion-savvy professionals who make predictions about future trends in fashion. Because their jobs involve predicting what is going to happen at a later date, what they do may sound a bit

At a Glance

Fashion Trend Forecaster

Minimum Educational Requirements
Bachelor's degree

Personal Qualities
Strong analytical skills, keen understanding of the fashion industry, business savvy, research skills, critical-thinking skills, excellent communication and interpersonal skills, in-depth knowledge of media (including social media)

Working Conditions
Inside an office and on the road; often long hours; high-pressure, fast-paced, continuously changing work environment; frequent travel

Salary Range
About $17,000 to $160,000

Number of Jobs
About 17,200 as of April 2018*

Future Job Outlook
Growth of 27 percent through 2026*

* Based on Bureau of Labor Statistics estimates for research analysts in retail industries

A fashion trend forecaster sifts through consumer buying behavior data, fashion trend reports, and fashion editorials. He will use this information, and additional research, to make predictions about fashion trends.

like fortune-telling. But the job is far more scientific than many people realize. As design editor David Nicholls writes in *House & Garden* online, "The professional trend forecaster is a far cry from the storybook old crone who makes crystal-ball predictions. In the same way that a meteorologist produces a weather forecast based on data from the atmosphere, a trend forecaster aims to extract tomorrow's tastes from the collected evidence of what is happening now."

The major task for trend forecasters is research—in every conceivable form. While going about their jobs, forecasters sift through staggering amounts of data as well as conduct a great deal of research of their own. They pore over information about consumer buying behaviors, fashion trend reports, and fashion editorials. They follow and study designer collections along with the fashions being featured at runway shows and how they are received. They interview fashion designers and boutique owners and talk with fashion-conscious people, famous as well as not famous, young as well as old. They travel to major cities throughout the world to learn what people are wearing and what the most popular trends are. These and other sources and techniques provide trend forecasters with a wealth of information. By synthesizing and analyzing it, while at the same time relying heavily on their instincts, they begin to spot patterns, and from there, they can start to make predictions about future fashion trends. "To me it's connecting the dots," says trend forecaster Sarah Owen in an article on the design and architecture website 99% Invisible. "It's pattern recognition. It's taking those cues and pairing that with [the] data that will kind of inform the future."

Over the years, fashion trend forecasting has changed drastically, and the main reason is the growth of the Internet. Social media especially has transformed how and where trend forecasters obtain their information. Jane Monnington Boddy, a veteran trend forecaster based in London, discusses this change in an interview on the Business of Fashion website. "There is a new strain of trend forecasting that has come about," says Boddy. "An influencer will post something on social media, like Kylie Jenner will wear something on Instagram, and two days later, you can buy it on [the online retailer] Boohoo. Or a girl band will wear lilac and 20,000 people like the post, so then a retailer will want to invest in lilac. It's a faster pace reaction—it's a fast-paced fashion—but it is trend forecasting at the end of the day because you are spotting these trends."

Owen is very familiar with the role social media plays in trendsetting. She works for World Global Style Network (WGSN), the world's largest trend forecasting company, which is headquartered in New York City. Owen was formerly in charge of forecasting the youth market. She spent an enormous amount of time on Instagram monitoring trends among young people, and in the process she became acquainted with a group of teenage girls. When it was time for the annual music and arts festival known as Coachella, Owen saw that the girls were talking about it on Instagram. So she connected with them and traveled to Palm Springs, California, to meet with them and learn more about their styles and what most influenced them. For the same reason, she attended a variety of other festivals throughout the United States, such as the Afropunk Festival in New York City. "I met the coolest people, got the best photos and asked about their style," says Owen in an interview on the Fashionista website. All these experiences helped Owen better understand the youth market and what styles were important to young people, so in turn, she could prepare reports for her clients.

Trend forecasting is valuable to numerous industries, but its roots and primary use are in fashion. The extensive reports created by trend forecasters, which are said to resemble Pinterest boards, provide guidance and inspiration to forecasters' clients. These include fashion designers, who use the data to decide on garment styles for a particular season; colorists, who mix, develop, and create color palettes for clothing and textiles; buyers and merchandisers, who rely on trend forecasting data to decide which fashions and accessories to buy for their stores; and other clients who have a vested interest in knowing what fashion trends to expect. The information clients glean from a trend forecaster's research can help guide them when making business decisions for the future.

How Do You Become a Fashion Trend Forecaster?

Education

Fashion trend forecasters typically earn a bachelor's degree, and they may choose different specialties. Merchandising, market research, and marketing are all business-focused programs that can give aspiring trend forecasters a good knowledge base. According to the Bureau of Labor Statistics (BLS), courses in statistics, research methods, and marketing are essential; other important classes include communications, economics, and consumer behavior.

Hands-On Experience

Aspiring fashion trend forecasters can benefit immensely from on-the-job experience, and that is a major benefit of internships. These are generally available to college students, are often paid, and usually take place during the summer months when students are on break. By interning, young people gain experience, gain knowledge from people working in the industry, gain new skills, make connections with company employees and potential clients, and have a valuable addition to their résumés. Another benefit of internships is that young people learn firsthand about a particular field, and that can help them decide whether it is really a career they want to pursue. If it is, the connections they make could lead to permanent employment.

Another good idea for aspiring trend forecasters is to start a blog. There is plenty of fashion-related data available that they can tap into and write about in blog posts. When they are interviewing for jobs, they can share what they have written with potential employers to show that they are passionate about their chosen career field.

Skills and Personality

In the interview on *Who What Wear*, Buckingham was asked about the top qualities she looks for when hiring people to work at Trendera, the marketing and trend forecasting company she founded in 2009. She replied, "Honesty. Resourcefulness. Kindness. Self-awareness. Interest in helping more than interest in being helped." In addition to those qualities, career experts emphasize the importance of keen analytical ability, critical-thinking skills, and excellent communication skills, including being an excellent listener as well as speaker. Trend forecasters must be knowledgeable about fashion and intrigued by changing styles and trends, as well as have a keen eye for detail. They must also be able to deal with a high-pressure environment and be flexible—because in their field, change is constant.

Employers

Fashion trend forecasters generally work for companies that specialize in trend forecasting. The largest of these employers is WGSN, which is headquartered in New York City and has branch offices in Los Angeles; London; Paris; Tokyo; Barcelona; Cape Town, South Africa; Verona, Italy; and Overath, Germany, as well as a number of other cities. Other trend forecasting companies include Trendera, with offices in Los Angeles and New York City; Doneger Group in New York City; Pantone in Carlstadt, New Jersey; Trendstop in London; and Promostyl in Paris. Another employment option for aspiring trend forecasters is working for major retailers that have their own forecasting staffs, such as Nordstrom, Macy's, and Urban Outfitters, among others.

Working Conditions

People who work in the field of fashion trend forecasting understand the meaning of *hectic* because it aptly describes their jobs. Trend forecasting is a competitive, fast-paced, and high-pressure career that requires hard work and long hours, so the job can be stressful. Trend forecasters spend time in their offices reviewing research, conducting analyses, and meeting with colleagues. They meet with clients for consultations and presentations. And often, their jobs require extensive travel, which means they are away from home a lot.

Earnings

According to the online employment marketplace ZipRecruiter, annual earnings for fashion trend forecasters range from a low of $17,000 to as high as $160,000 as of March 2019. Salaries can vary widely, depending on geographic location, years of experience, and employer.

Opportunities for Advancement

As they gain experience and knowledge, fashion trend forecast-ers can advance in their careers to higher-level positions. Most choose to work for large trend forecasting firms because there are more opportunities, while others prefer smaller, boutique-style firms. As with any career, the ability to advance often depends on how hard an employee is willing to work. In the interview with *Who What Wear*, Buckingham offers these words: "Young people should focus more on what they can do for the company than what the company can do for them. In turn, then the company will see that, and their bosses will see that."

What Is the Future Outlook for Fashion Trend Forecasters?

The BLS does not collect data for trend forecasters, but it does collect data for market research analysts for the retail industry, which is not the same career but is comparable. According to a BLS report dated April 13, 2018, the projected growth for mar-ket research analysts is extremely promising: 27 percent through 2026, which equates to forty-seven hundred new jobs that will become available in the coming years.

Find Out More

Business of Fashion
website: www.businessoffashion.com

The Business of Fashion website publishes articles related to the fashion and beauty industry. Content includes a daily digest, in-formation about fashion and technology, and a podcast. Under the website's "Education" section are online courses, industry advice, and advice for college applicants.

EDITED
website: https://edited.com

The EDITED website is the most extensive source of real-time retail data in the world. It provides insights on fashion trends on the basis of the work of both retail merchandisers and data scientists. Users can subscribe through the EDITED website to access newsletters, as well as promotions from various brands and retailers.

Trend Council
430 W. Twenty-Fourth St., Suite 1B
New York, NY 10011
website: http://trendcouncil.com

Trend Council is a design tool for designers, buyers, and manufacturers intended to take the guesswork out of trend forecasting. It offers sample reports for users on everything from denim to colors to accessories. Visitors to its website can sign up for virtual demos and weekly emails with updates on the latest fashion trends.

World Global Style Network (WGSN)
229 W. Forty-Third St., Seventh Floor
New York, NY 10036
website: www.wgsn.com

The WGSN is an organization of trend forecasters that provides insights for designers and buyers, among others. Its website includes a blog, press releases, and information about trade shows. The website also includes information on trends in fashion, beauty, and lifestyle.

Fashion Photographer

What Does a Fashion Photographer Do?

When members of the fashion-loving public see striking photos of models wearing the latest fashions, they are looking at the creations of fashion photographers. These talented, artistic professionals shoot photos for magazine features, newspaper fashion spreads, online fashion publications, fashion catalogs, retail clothing stores, and stock photos. One of them is Lindsay Adler, a New York City photographer who was named one of the top-ten fashion photographers in the world.

Adler's photos have been featured in and on the covers of *Vogue*, *Elle*, *Marie Claire*, and *In-Style*, as well as other leading fashion publications. In an interview with the online photography magazine PHLEARN, Adler talks about her background and how she came to specialize in fashion photography. "Since I first picked up a camera, I've tried just about every type of photography out there," she says. "In my early teens, I started by photographing nature and landscapes. In high school, I focused on traditional

At a Glance

Fashion Photographer

Minimum Educational Requirements
None

Personal Qualities
Artistic talent, imagination, keen eye for detail, strong interest in fashion, good interpersonal skills, organizational skills

Working Conditions
In a studio or on location, inside or outside; typically long, irregular hours; heavy lifting of photography equipment; long periods of standing

Salary Range
About $29,479 to more than $80,000

Number of Jobs
About 2,300 as of 2016*

Future Job Outlook
Growth of 9.6 percent through 2026*

* Based on Bureau of Labor Statistics estimates for photographers specializing in arts, entertainment, and recreation

portraiture. In college, I tried my hand at photojournalism." As Adler continued to gain experience, she found that fashion photography was where she belonged. "When I first tried my hand at fashion photography," she says, "I felt an excitement and passion that I had never felt before."

Most people know that the work lives of fashion photographers revolve around photo shoots. But many have no idea of the huge amount of planning that must take place for a fashion photo shoot to come together. In the online magazine *Phoblographer*, Los Angeles fashion photographer Derrick Freske discusses the preshoot planning phase, which can take days and involves countless details. Freske explains, "For a recent job I had to send emails, hop on a few phone calls, look over a project brief, location scout, organize a shot list, find an assistant to help me with lighting, organize hair/makeup/styling, and cast models. This isn't how every client shoot is, but it gives you an idea of everything that goes on behind the scenes to make the photos you see in advertisements!"

On the day of a photo shoot, fashion photographers assume the role of director. They ensure that the schedule, which has been prepared ahead of time, is strictly adhered to. They check lighting at all different angles, because proper lighting is critical for creating the appropriate mood. They work with a stylist to get the models ready and posed, and when all these steps are complete, the photographing can begin. According to Adler, as professional as a photo shoot must be, the people involved should be able to enjoy themselves. "The days of my shoots are a fantastic mix of serious and fun," she says in the PHLEARN interview. "We are all serious about our art, sticking to the schedule, executing the vision. That being said, we have an amazing time and are flexible enough to allow us to create openly. We eat great food, listen to music, laugh, tell stories, shoot funny behind the scenes, and just create an environment for open expression."

Not all fashion photo shoots are the same. Some are chaotic because they take place at a live event rather than in a studio where everything is meticulously controlled. This is certainly true of Fashion Week, which is held in February and September each year in New York City, London, Paris, and Milan. The fashion shows during the weeklong event are glamorous, star-studded affairs—but the photographers face a daunting task. "It's a lot of hard work and a lot of waiting around," says fashion photographer Andrew H. Walker in an interview with the online photography magazine *PDNedu*. Walker is a veteran Fashion Week photographer; in February 2019 he photographed his tenth in New York City. He says there are three types of assignments at these fashion shows: backstage before a show starts, the runway during the show, and photographing front-row celebrities.

The backstage photography is the most relaxed, and photographers have an opportunity to be creative and have a little fun. They can capture models getting their hair and makeup done, photograph the fashion designers attending to details of their designs, and show the models relaxing before it is time for them to walk the runway. When the show starts, however, relaxation time is over. According to Walker, shooting the runway activity is the most technically challenging. "'It's completely 'do-or-die,'" he says. Walker adds that there are two things a photographer absolutely must do for runway shooting to be successful: make sure camera settings are accurate, and be strategically positioned on the runway. "Once the lights go down and the show begins," he says, "you have a few seconds per model to get all of the shots: full-length, half-length, headshot, plus shoes and/or accessories."

By far the toughest part of the Fashion Week assignment, says Walker, is photographing famous fashion show attendees. "Shooting the front row celebrities is simply mayhem," he says, "particularly if they are A-list celebrities." During that time a photographer's goal is to get full-length photos of what the celebrities are wearing, as well as shots of them sitting together. And that is no simple task, because multiple photographers are on the runway at the same time, all to capture their own photos. Yet as challenging as the Fashion Week assignment is, Walker still enjoys himself. "My favorite part is the challenge of entering an entirely different situation every day and figuring out how to make strong images."

Education

According to the job resource website Career Trend, there are typically no education requirements for fashion photographers. Many who aspire to a fashion photography career do, however, go to college and earn a bachelor's degree. They may choose an art-related major, like graphic design, visual arts, or photography, or choose a major that is unrelated to art.

In the interview with PHLEARN magazine, Adler says that she earned three college degrees from Syracuse University: one in political science, one in business, and one in visual communications. Despite her education, though, Adler says that she does not believe college is essential for a photographer. "What is essential is the drive to learn and educate yourself," she says. "You can gain an education working for another photographer, or attending workshops and seminars, or simply by experimentation. Some people need the structure of college to help them focus and refine their vision. If you have the passion and drive, you will make it happen with or without a degree."

Hands-On Experience

With her reference to experimentation, Adler is emphasizing the importance of learning by doing—shooting photography at every possible opportunity in order to gain knowledge and experience. Photographers overwhelmingly agree that the more aspiring photographers practice their craft, the better they will become and the more opportunities will open to them.

This is what Freske did. He grew up in a small town in Michigan and dropped out of college after three years to go to Los Angeles and attempt to make it as a fashion photographer. He shot photo after photo after photo before he left Michigan and after he arrived in Los Angeles, and he posted his work on Instagram, where he gradually built up a large following. Armed with an impressive portfolio of his photography, Freske aggressively

Before a fashion shoot, a photographer works with his team to adjust the lighting and scenery. Lighting, scenery, and staging all contribute to the photographer's ability to highlight the best features of the client's fashions.

pursued clients in Los Angeles and started getting assignments. When he talks to young people now, he emphasizes how absolutely essential it is to "practice, practice, practice!," as he says during the *Phoblographer* interview. "Photography takes time and doesn't happen overnight. . . . Back when I was first starting off, I would take a new photo every day to keep improving my skills. Ask your friends or family if you can take photos of them or you can do what I did when I first started off and take self portraits."

Skills and Personality

Fashion photographers are, by nature, artistic and imaginative people. In order to succeed in this career, they need a keen eye for detail, a strong interest in fashion, and good organizational skills. People skills are also essential for fashion photographers because they regularly interact with models, stylists, photography crew members, and others involved in planning and executing photo shoots. They also need patience and the ability to remain calm in chaotic situations, such as photographing fashion shows. And because most photographers work as freelancers, they need business and marketing skills.

On the Job

Employers
According to the Bureau of Labor Statistics (BLS), nearly 70 percent of professional photographers are self-employed. Those who do not work for themselves may be employed by photography studios, advertising agencies, or fashion publications.

Working Conditions
A fashion photographer's work life is unpredictable—and so is the work environment, which varies considerably, depending on what is taking place. When planning a photo shoot, photographers spend many hours in the office. Photo shoots can take place almost anywhere, from inside the photographer's studio to outdoors at a tropical beach to a glitzy, crowded, event-packed fashion show. The hours are often long, the work is often tiring, and it can be very difficult to lug around heavy camera equipment for hours at a time. Yet despite the drawbacks, many fashion photographers have no desire to change careers. As Walker says in the *PDNedu* interview: "At the end of the day, even an exhausting one, I'd rather be doing this than anything else."

Earnings
According to the salary and benefits website PayScale, the annual earnings for fashion photographers range from $29,479 to more than $80,000. Salaries often vary widely, depending on the photographer's experience and reputation, the client's budget, and geographic location. In the PHLEARN interview, Adler shares her thoughts about earnings: "I am not a photographer because of a desire to make money. I could choose a wide range of other careers if my focus was purely on making money.

I am a photographer because it is my passion and expressing my vision through personal work is one of the most rewarding things in my life."

Opportunities for Advancement
Fashion photographers who have achieved success have worked hard to prove themselves and establish their reputations. So for them, career advancement means getting the premier fashion photography assignments that they covet, while continuing to grow professionally and being free to pursue their artistic passions.

What Is the Future Outlook for Fashion Photographers?

The BLS collects data on photographers but not specifically on fashion photographers. The closest category is photographers who specialize in arts, entertainment, and recreation. For that specialty, the BLS projects 9.6 percent growth through 2026, which is faster than the average for all occupations.

Find Out More

American Society of Media Photographers (ASMP)
PO Box 31207
Bethesda, MD 20824
website: www.asmp.org

The ASMP is a trade organization for the world's top media photographers, including fashion photographers. Its website includes a blog, a magazine, and information about events for members. Membership in the ASMP comes with a host of benefits, including a listing in its Find a Photographer database and access to ASMP publications.

Association of Photographers Ltd. (AOP)
8–10 Sampson St.
London E1W 1NA
United Kingdom
website: www.the-aop.org

The AOP is an organization for anyone interested in working as a photographer, including professionals, students, and those just starting out in the industry. Membership benefits for students include an e-newsletter, photography workshops and events, how-to guides, and sample forms for practice running a photography business.

National Press Photographers Association (NPPA)
120 Hooper St.
Athens, GA 30602
website: https://nppa.org

The NPPA is a membership organization for students, freelancers, part-timers, and professionals working as photographers. For a yearly fee, students can access a subscription to its *News Photographer* magazine, a mentorship program, a listing in the NPPA professional directory, and a jobs board.

Society of International Fashion and
Glamour Photographers (SIFGP)
6 Bath St.
Rhyl LL18 3EB
United Kingdom
website: www.sifgp.com

The SIFGP is a professional organization for fashion and glamour photographers. Its website includes information about SIFGP photography competitions and a yearly photography convention and trade show. By becoming a member, students and aspiring professionals gain access to a private forum, a listing on the SIFGP website, and a place to showcase photography work.

Interview with a Fashion Stylist

Basia Richard is a fashion stylist in Los Angeles who has worked as a stylist for more than fifteen years. Well known for her unique, chic, and timeless style, Richard has worked with a number of celebrities, including Selena Gomez, Bella Thorne, Irina Shayk, Olivia Holt, and Hilary Duff, among others. For Gomez, Richard helped create looks for her editorial spreads, music videos, concert tours, red carpet appearances, and album covers. In an interview conducted by email, Richard provided answers to the author's questions.

Q: Why did you become a fashion stylist?
A: Before I got into the fashion industry, I had no idea that the job even existed. It was over fifteen years ago when I started and I didn't know much about it. But I always loved fashion. Growing up in Poland, I would read all the fashion magazines and I was very fascinated by the fashion business. I was studying to become a concert violinist. When I moved to the United States, that's what I thought I would be doing. Then a friend asked me to dress him for one of the award galas in Los Angeles and I loved it so much that I kind of knew at that very moment that I wanted to pursue a career in fashion.

Q: Can you describe your typical workday?
A: My typical day is never the same. It all depends what I am working on. I might be shopping all day, pulling clothes for upcoming jobs, doing a lot of research online, sending request emails to publicists for an upcoming Red Carpet job, working

71

on set on different locations or sometimes organizing my studio, advance styling for upcoming jobs and viewing new collections. A lot of things happen at the last minute and it's very difficult to plan anything ahead of time.

Q: What is it like to work with celebrities?
A: I was never star struck, so for me, I have always treated it as a job. Some of them are demanding and some are very easygoing so that all depends. Most of the stars I have worked with are very charismatic and sure of themselves—in a good way.

Q: What do you like most about your job?
A: I like the fact that I am privileged to work with some of the most talented people like directors and photographers who inspire me with their creativity. I also love working on locations and I worked on many amazing jobs where I had a chance to travel and spend time in beautiful mansions and amazing outdoor locations.

Q: What do you like least about your job?
A: I think the most difficult part is that all my jobs come at the last minute and I can't plan anything in advance.

Q: What personal qualities do you find most valuable for your line of work?
A: Flexibility, strong organizational skills, being able to work on many projects in the same time, having a strong personality, critical thinking, ability to work under high pressure.

Q: What is the best way to prepare to become a fashion stylist?
A: I actually created an online course on how to become a fashion and celebrity stylist since I couldn't find anything out there that would educate and prepare the next generation to get in this industry. I invite aspiring fashion stylists to visit https://mystylist academy.com to see if this career might interest them.

Also, hands-on experience is everything in the fashion styling world, and a great way to get that experience is by participating in internships. When I interned for a stylist, I got to work with celebrities like Jeremy Piven and Christina Aguilera. Afterward I started to put my portfolio together, and could start getting my own clients and my own styling jobs. Aspiring stylists should always look into internships.

Q: What other advice do you have for students who might be interested in this career?
A: Get a college degree—and it doesn't need to be in a fashion specialty. Be persistent, work very hard, and make connections. Styling . . . is one of the most interesting and fascinating jobs to work in and totally worth it to pursue.

Other Jobs in Fashion

Art director
Boutique owner
Brand representative
Clothing pattern maker
Costume designer
Fabric librarian
Fashion account executive
Fashion colorist
Fashion coordinator
Fashion editorial assistant
Fashion merchandiser
Fashion model agent
Fashion publicist
Fashion public relations
    specialist
Fashion sales representative

Fit model
Garment technologist
Graphic designer
Hair stylist
Junior visual merchandiser
Lingerie designer
Makeup artist
Pattern maker
Product manager
Retail salesperson
Runway model
Sample maker
Showroom manager
Social media assistant
Textile designer
Textile fabric colorist

Editor's note: The US Department of Labor's Bureau of Labor Statistics provides information about hundreds of occupations. The agency's *Occupational Outlook Handbook* describes what these jobs entail, the work environment, education and skill requirements, pay, future outlook, and more. The *Occupational Outlook Handbook* may be accessed online at www.bls.gov/ooh.

Index

Picture Credits

Cover: g-stockstudio/iStockphoto

6: Maury Aaseng

11: g-stockstudio/Shutterstock.com

29: monkeybusinessimages/iStock

56: baranq/Shutterstock.com

67: jacoblund/iStock

About the Author

Peggy J. Parks has written dozens of educational books on a wide variety of topics for children, teens, and young adults. She holds a bachelor's degree from Aquinas College in Grand Rapids, Michigan, where she graduated magna cum laude. Parks lives in Muskegon, Michigan, a town she says inspires her writing because of its location on the shores of beautiful Lake Michigan.